Life itself is vanishing fast.
Make haste for eternity.

~ **Robert E. Murray**

"The rhythm of Life is intricate but orderly;
tenacious but fragile,
to keep that in mind
is to hold the key to survival."

~ **Judge Shirley**

Also by Kamal Parmar

Still Waters ('Silver Bow Publishing)
Just Passing By (Silver Bow Publishing)

Vanishing Into The Blue

Kamal Parmar

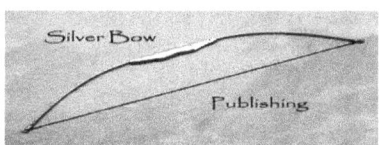

720 – Sixth Street, Box # 5
New Westminster, BC
V3C 3C5   CANADA

Title: Vanishing Into The Blue
Author: Kamal Parmar
Publisher: Silver Bow Publishing
Cover Art: "Moonlight" painting by Candice James
Layout/Design/Editing: Candice James

All rights reserved including the right to reproduce or translate this book or any portions thereof, in any form without the permission of the publisher. Except for the use of short passages for review purposes, no part of this book may be reproduced, in part or in whole, or transmitted in any form or by any means, either by means electronically or mechanically, including photocopying, recording, or any information or storage retrieval system without prior permission in writing from the publisher.

ISBN: 978-1-77403- paperback
ISBN: 978-1-77403- e- book

© Silver Bow Publishing 2024

Library and Archives Canada Cataloguing in Publication

Title: Vanishing into the blue / Kamal Parmar.
Names: Parmar, Kamal, 1953- author.
Description: Poems.
Identifiers: Canadiana (print) 20240316886 | Canadiana (ebook) 20240316894 | ISBN 9781774032930
   (softcover) | ISBN 9781774032947 (Kindle)
Subjects: LCGFT: Poetry.
Classification: LCC PS8631.A765 V36 2024 | DDC C811/.6—dc23

Acknowledgement

I am deeply indebted to my family for having the patience to bear with me during my rendezvous with the Muse.

My special thanks to my publisher, Candice James, of Silver Bow publishing for having *polished* these poems.

Vanishing into the Blue

CONTENTS

Listening To Fall / 9
A Park Comes To Life / 11
Shimmering Pond / 12
They Call It Fall / 13
A Roseate Dawn / 14
The First Snowfall / 16
Spring Knocks / 17
Winter Stillness / 18
Time Is Passing / 19
Seascape / 20
Early Dawn / 21
Day Break / 23
Days Gone By / 24
Still Silent Twilight / 25
Bewitched / 26
A Trail To Nowhere / 28
Joy's Of A Winter's Hearth / 29
Searching / 30
Is It Spring? / 32
Ushering In Twilight / 34
Fleeting Time / 36
Unfolding Summer / 37
Waiting For Fall / 38
The Tide Of Life / 40
Is It Really Fall? / 42
Harvest Moon / 44
Mystic Moon / 45
Crescent Moon / 46
Night Watch / 47
Lo And Behold! / 48
Night Sky / 50
The Breath Of Autumn / 51
Wintry Dusk / 53
The First Snowfall / 54

Look To This Day! / 55
An Evening To Remember / 57
The Pulse Of Winter / 59
Still Summer Sky / 60
The First Blush / 61
Magic Of A Summer Night / 62
Vanishing Into The Blue / 63

Listening To Fall

    Listen to the Fall.
      talk to the trees;
the soaring arbutus, furry cypress,
and the shaggy headed oak,
whose sprawling shadows
stretch across silent valleys.

    I hear no words,
      their soft whispers
drowned by the sighing breeze

except their muted tongues,
tinged with the woody smell
    of cedar and pine.

A lonely road winds like a thread
stitching the quilted landscape,
blazing with bright yellow and ochre,
glinting in the early morning sunrays.

There is a silence so deep
that can be felt in your bones,
in every breath of the earth
as it floats in the cosmos.

Drenched with dawn,
silent valleys open their bosoms
to embrace the world.

Sparrows chirp, swoop low,
then rise on cushions of air,
to circumvent the arbutus
and wild bramble bush.
A raw cry of a raven echoes
      across the rising morning mist.
The distant hum of a car dissolves
      into the darkness.

The air is filled
with leaves of maple and birch
that dance like carefree damsels
to celebrate the colours of Fall.

A Park Comes To Life

Tucked beside a clump of pines and cypress,
      a park comes to life.
Its swings and slides stand out
in vibrant reds and shimmering pink.
It is quiet, except for the swish of the breeze
blowing through the cypress.

At sundown, when shadows lengthen,
a gentle summer breeze caresses the leaves.
      The park comes alive
with the giggles and shouts of children,
echoing across the quiet neighborhood
   and the ivy tufted roofs of homes.

A
 Perhaps he is turning back
   the man with a walking cane
shuffles along the winding path,
stops and waves at little Jane
in curly hair and pigtails.

He sighs, and gazes at the sky.

chapters of his Life,
     mellow with age,
those days of yore, of fun and frolic,
   when life was chock-full
of surprises and excitement.

Little did he know , what lay ahead...

     A lonely life
  spent talking to his shadow
  in a one room apartment,
  that echoed with his sighs.

Shimmering Pond

At the far end of our garden lies a pond,
hidden behind clumps of overgrown bramble-bush,
straddling across the trodden muddy path,
that meanders and disappears into nowhere.

A weeping willow lies tacked to it.
Its slender branches dance like ballerinas,
when the Fall breeze sings sweet nothings to them.

In the smouldering western sky, the pond shimmers,
      sending ripples across its length.

      A lone willow stands solitary,
silhouetted in the approaching darkness.
It's almost twilight and a church bell rings.

      It's time for evening prayers.
     A gentle hush descends.

A shrill cry of a raven tears across the heavens,
     as the evening star beckons.
 and the pond shivers under a twilight sky.

I watch with bated breath,
see summer slowly fading away,
as Fall surreptitiously tiptoes in.

They Call It Fall

Listen to the cascading music of a cool breeze,
rising from a gentle whisper to a gusty wind:
like the ebb and tide of an ocean wave,
like the highs and lows of an opera singer,
like curve balls that manifest on Life's journey.

It picks up speed, swirls its invisible cape
between maple and cherry branches,
    sucking out their leaves,
leaving stark and bony skeletons behind.

I stand under a canopy of interlocking branches
stitched by leaves of flaming yellows and reds;
a stark contrast to the deep blue cloud mottled sky.

My laughter echoes through the pebbled streets,
lined with piles and piles of crinkled maple leaves,
    skittering along curbs,
with the magnetic pull of the Fall fairy,
painting a canvas of maple and arbutus,
      yellow and rust
    with its invisible brush.

    As far as the eye can see,
    rolling valleys are a flaming gold,
hemmed with blotches of russet and brown bush.

    All the while, the blurry sun watches,
as shadows gallop and linger; then cross, in silence.

A Roseate Dawn

Eerie and mystical,
the veil of winter night lifts,
    oh, so gently,
revealing a quilted landscape of white,
dimpled and pock marked.

The snow refuses to melt,
as winter's icy grip tightens its hold.
Frigid cypress and stately pines
stand as rigid sentinels,
silent and sighing —
an ode to the cold season.

The morning is quiet,
except for the soft stirring of crispy breeze
that stirs the snow dusted branches of the trees,
    then dies down,
swallowed by a stillness that lingers,
   throughout the silent valley,
dotted with a few houses,
half-buried under the snow that fell last night.

Nothing seems astir —
semi-frozen ponds glisten,
bulrushes stand cold and rigid.
Pugmarks on snow, so soft and deep,
maybe of a fawn that has lost its way,
or an Arctic fox awaking from hibernation.

Up above, the sky is no longer star sprayed.
The North Star still twinkles but now, faintly,
as the wintry light nudges the night away.
First beams of sunlight fan out in the east,
squint through the arbutus and fir,
bathing the cedar in gold
to the make the clouds blush-
just to whisper,-*'it's a new day.'*

Far out near the horizon,
where the ocean meets the sky,
the scintillating glare of the morning sun
sets the ocean waters ablaze.
Its ripples glinting gold.

Day ebbs to dusk
as soft waves move
like rhythmic folds of silk,
their sheen reflecting a new morn.

The First Snowfall

In the pale glimmer of moonlight,
the landscape lies still,
quilted in soft white snow
that had fallen all day,
transforming Nanaimo into a winter fairy land.
The dimpled earth is strangely quiet,
      as if in meditation.

Curls of smoke arise from my floral coffee mug,

I look up at the horizon.
Frigid arbutus stand naked,
snow dusted conifers and cypress
taper towards a grey somber sky
that spells drifting snow.

Snow speckled hills arise, as if to say something,
but their tongues are, muted.
Mist swaddled Mount Benson arises,
stately with its white cape,
while the West coast lies in quiet slumber
dreaming of summer, that ilies sleeping in the past.

      There is silence,
    an expectancy,
     a stillness
casting a magic spell on me,
    drawing me closer.

I look wide-eyed, mesmerized
  by this winter wonderland.

Spring Knocks

       In early spring,
when the snow thaws and ponds glisten,
when the wren wakes up from its slumber
    and chipmunks are astir—
  tender petals of tulips uncurl.

Winds blow through
the naked willow and silver birch,
to nudge them awake
and breathe life into
the knobby cherry blossom tree.

There is a tear in the cloud mottled sky
revealing the powdery blue tint of spring.
I still feel the frosty breath of winter,
even though spring is at my doorstep.
Frost ringed dewdrops still glisten
on the cusp of a lily leaf,
glittering pearls of joy;
the day in a microcosm.

I remember last year,
when spring had just arrived
and the sandy beach lay soft and smooth,
dimpled with footprints of yesterday's revellers.
Empty coke cans half buried in sand,
a pink beach ball caught in the weeds at low tide.
Moments to savour and hang on to,
speechless with bliss.

Now the long wait has ended,
   days are getting longer
   and happiness unfolds
     like a tulip bud.

Winter Stillness

Sitting in the warm glow of the fireplace,
our faces mirror the flicker of the flames,
      their tongues leaping up.

      I sip coffee.
the crackling and hissing of the flames,
      the only sound of winter.

      I look outside my window,
every tree, bush and scrub, is pearly white,
      pure and pristine,
   as though in meditation.

      A cold breeze starts up,
like the sighing of the forgotten souls of the Past,
      a past lost in oblivion,
   buried in deep recesses of my mind.

A silent prayer escapes from my lips,
   although my tongue is muted.

Glancing through the lace curtains of my window,
   I see the frigid air filled with falling snow.

      No respite from winter.

Time Is Passing

Rain pours white,
drumming on snow splattered rooftops,
smattering on window panes,
refusing to let go.

Slowly, inch by inch,
white tufts of meringue-shaped snow
melt away, shrinking
to become shallow puddles of water,
with the rain washed sky in them.
The day in a microcosm.

In our backyard,
the snow still lingers
looking like shreds of frayed linen,
to pockmark the grassy stubble.

The sombre sky veiled
by a filigree of birch and conifers.

What does it say?

Time is passing,
nothing lasts forever.
Soon, Spring will arrive,
our hopes unwavering.

Seascape

Distant mountains rise against a sombre sky,
blotchy grey, with clouds
that float like silent dreams.

Down below, the ocean sleeps
like a mercurial mirror shining brilliant.

Up above, a few sea-gulls twirl and swirl
on cushions of air, soft and balmy,
like kites without strings.

The eerie silence snuffs out the hollow cry
of a seagull, swooping down
towards the algae-laced waters
licking the shore.

A barge looms in sight, like a ghost
silhouetted in the misty horizon,
glinting streaks of silver
herald the crescent of a moon
that peeps from behind a cumulus cloud.

Lone star silently watches.

Early Dawn

At the first streaks of dawn,
a soft grey light creeps stealthily
across the eastern sky,
gently lifting the veil of the dark night,
A few stars still linger,
refusing to let go off their milky light
that had bathed the Universe, all night.

A sliver of a moon is still etched in the sky,
paled by the ethereal glow of Dawn.

Night has become a thing of the Past,
leaving shards of memories behind.

      Realities melt into dreams.
Dreams that seem to evaporate into thin air,
        erased forever.

      Drawing aside my frilly curtain,
I can see the scraggly outline of the cedars and pines,
    dotted with houses bundled together,
      peeping through the forest glade,
        so strangely quiet.

Then something happens—
the valley is suddenly bathed in light,
brilliant and glowing,
as if touched by an invisible wand of the Fairy.

Shafts of sunlight slant through
the shaggy cypress and slender arbutus,
squinting across wild rhododendrons
    and wispy dandelions,
to fan over rooftops of silent cottages,
then to kiss the silent waters
      of a still pond,
that shatters into a thousand sparkles,

mirroring the newly born day,
so fresh and pure.

I feel a strange sensation come over me,
a wave of euphoria washing me off my feet,
taking me higher and higher
into a realm of happiness.

I feel joy coursing through my veins.

      I am speechless.
        I am joy.

Daybreak

A snow-smothered village sleeps,
amidst a quilted landscape of snowbanks.
Mounds of snow with frozen ponds and frigid lakes
dot the somnolent wintery earth.

In the far east, a chink of light peeps gingerly,
the first skeins of dawn visible,
a spark of a newborn day,
fresh and pure as the first breath of life,
as a shiny dewdrop.
Ice-crystal laced bulrushes
skirt still waters of hidden pools and clinging moss.

Daylight creeps in,
squints through a filigree of naked arbutus,
silhouetting their curvaceous and slender trunks.

    Up above, a swallow sweeps low,
  folding the morning light in its wings.

        Ah! the joy of freedom.

Days Gone By

Time flies.
Just the other day,
I was a shy, gawky girl
holding my mother's hand,
sometimes, hiding behind my mother's back.

The other times, clinging to her apron,
an excuse to miss school that day.

What fun to laze around at home,
chase butterflies and pluck marigolds,
flashing yellow in the afternoon sun.
This was bliss.

Those joyful days of childhood,
    have gone forever,
to become a long lost dream
that I relive over and over again
    and drown into euphoria,
        fuelled by nostalgia.

Still Silent Twilight

Neither light nor night.
The sky, grey as a pigeon,
mourns the sober day,
frigid and cold.

Trees cotton-balled with clods of snow
stand mute and numb.
The road, snaking and soul-less,
swallowed by the approaching darkness.
Cottages tucked in a valley,
a cocoon of pearly white.

Ponds no longer shimmer,
bulrushes no longer dance,
they stand like faceless sentinels.

Solitary lampposts
shed accordions of pale light
across curb-less lanes.
Silence is hypnotic,
washes me off my feet
like a wave engulfing my body and soul.

There are no sparrows
flying homeward to their mates,
no night jars or the old barn owl hooting.

A cold night awaits
in the wings of a brooding sky.
It is the first night of winter.
I am drawn towards it.

        Its quietude –
a magic potion that I could drink forever
  and drown into a fountain of bliss.

Bewitched

      A mid-summer night
heavy with the smell of honeysuckle,
        enticing.

I lay my head on a soft tuft of green grass
        encircling a pond.

Sleep does not come to me.
I watch the starry spectacle up above,
blink at me in unison,
Other times, they leave a sparkling trail
of shooting stars that spiral
into the mysterious Unknown.
Could be the Orion or Andromeda glaxaies,
melting into the Milky way.

A cool breeze washes over me.
The silence casts a spell on me.
Yet, all is not quiet nor still. I close my eyes
and a cacophony of sounds drowns me.
A rustle under the wild gooseberry bush,
perhaps a sparrow snuggling close to its babies,
a sudden flapping of wings among the bulrushes,
maybe a night jar looking for his mate.

A shrill cry of a raven shatters the stillness,
on having a close encounter with an old barn owl,
perched on a weeping willow tree
overhanging the quiet pond.\

A family of crickets chirps,
flits from one fern bush to another.

In the far distance,
a distant hum of a car speeds away,.
oblivious to everything around us.

Nature's orchestra breaks into a chorus
then rises towards the heavens,
towards the stars and the worlds beyond,
         seamless.

     A sudden hush falls
      and the starlit dome
shimmers and twinkles in applause.

     I am ... bewitched .

A Trail To Nowhere

I have walked this muddy trail,
with its serpentine pathways
hugging the cypress trees.

I have been mesmerized
by the magic spell of a waterfall,
tumbling under the star-washed pale night sky.

I hold my breath as I watch
the silvery glint of water
under a half-moon brooding up above.

I have opened my arms to embrace
the soft gush of summer breeze
wrapping around the lone willow
that stands near the stables.

I have stopped in my tracks,
to pluck a trillium peep at me,
under a bramble bush.

I have knelt down to kiss wild daisies,
      as they nodded at me
skirting a meandering cobbled pathway.

I had a wonderful time, just me and mom.
Now, I walk alone, just me and my shadow.

      The path may look barren,
        but to me, it blooms,
exuding a fragrance of sweet memories.

Joys Of A Winter's Hearth

We sit around the wood fire
as it crackles and hisses,
spits out curls of smoke
that dissolve and melt into
the inky darkness of the night.

Hot flames leap , curling and licking
    the searing wooden logs,
        the air ... heavy
with the smell of cedar and pine.

Our faces glow in the flicker
of the sparkling flames.
Their leaping tongues will soon turn
the chopped logs to dying embers
    and grey feathery ash.

        We sit snug, hanging onto
        our Starbucks steaming lattes.

Someone strums on a guitar,
picks out the chords and hums a tune
that resonates with the heartbeat of Mother earth.

The shaggy headed pines stand spellbound ,
      with muted tongues.

      Silent spectres of Joy

Searching

Where do I begin?
      There is no beginning.
Where do I end?
T   There is no ending.

I looked for you in rolling grasslands,
searched desperately in mist wrapped valleys,
the air laced with lavender.

      I could not find you,
      not even a trace of you.
      Yet, I never gave up.

I looked for you
in the early hours of dawn
before the first rays of the sun
set the slanting roofs of hamlets on fire.

I looked for you in the twilight sky,
in the still hour when the evening star
had still not risen,

I looked for you in the star spangled night sky,
then across the valley
where dark galloping shadows of the pines
stretch into oblivion —
your whereabouts still not known.

Helpless, I decide to walk on a muddy path
dotted with tiny cottages.
Morning sunlight fans across
the balmy summer breeze,
silhouetting the ferns and blueberry bushes.

There is a hypnotic hush,
as if in salutation to the Dawn.
I walk on.

The crunch of footsteps catches my attention,
a faint strumming of a guitar,
its chords float toward the sky,
like celestial notes from heaven.

I stop in my tracks.
Someone is crooning a song.
The soft words cascade toward me.

The world rings out with musical tones
        rising to a crescendo.
The sky sings, while the earth dances.

        Now I know,
    I had finally found you,
        hiding within me,
all the time, waiting to be unravelled,
a perfume to be spread all around me.

        Happiness —
a treasure to be cherished forever.

        Priceless and free.

Is it Spring?

I peep through my bedroom window.
A tangled web of silver birch branches
stands tall behind our soaring condo.

Stark naked, like a mesh of capillaries,
a spider's web spawns the pale blue sky.

        I wonder,
    is Spring really here?

I saunter out wearing my faded jeans
and blue denim jacket.
The silence, drowned by the 'crunch-crunch'
of my sneakers holds my attention,
as if the grass and the almost opal sky
is sharing a secret with me ...
        A secret I know not.

I look around me, blueberry bushes look the same.
A pink wild rose stares at me blankly.
A few curls of lily leaves seem to stand out,

Just a few sprigs of green, I tell myself.

        I walk on.
The path winds, dissolving into a dense canopy
        of conifers and firs.
Sunlight squints through chinks of the forest,

A wren flits past, swoops low
and takes off along my path,
as if beckoning me to follow it.
A magnetic pull draws me towards it.
I turn the corner, reach a dead end,
look askance through the corner of my eye,
a valley unfolds in front of me,
an embroidered carpet of blooming flowers.

Bright yellow faces of daffodils, little cusps of narcissus
dance in the breeze, smile at me.

    I stand entranced

I inhale the heady fragrance of hyacinth,
as Spring awaits in the wings of the day.

Ushering In Twilight

Far out in the west,
the sun has long gone,
reclining on a bed of fading scarlet and red.

Evening light becomes fainter;
it is neither day nor night —
      it is twilight.

Rolling hills and reclining valleys
are bathed in mystic mauves
as a veil of mist rolls in,
to wrap the furry silhouettes of pines
in its embrace.

There is a strange silence,
so captivating and serene.

      I close my eyes,
feel my heartbeat and earth's as one,
resonating with the synchronised movement
of sun, moon and earth.

     There is a wing flutter of starlings,
little specks that swoop low and then rise up ,
      gliding over cushions of air,
like the gentle crest and trough of ocean waves,
       to fan out into oblivion.

     All is quiet and still again.

In the pale light of the dying day,
when the sun is long gone
and nights awaits,
a pale silvery sliver of moon
glints through the tiny chinks
between the leafy poplars
gently swaying in the twilight breeze.

A heady fragrance of honeysuckle fills the air,
       intoxicating me.

      Soon the traffic will thin out,
      the winding road will dissolve
      and the noise of speeding cars,
      will be swallowed in silence.

Fleeting Time

Time slips away.
I slide and glide
clinging onto mellow memories,
some blurry and others unfading,
like the heady fragrance of lavender
that lingers and lingers ... on and on.

I look in the mirror.
I see a face wrinkled and sagging.
Eyes that once sparkled
are now shallow pools of light.

What happened?
Is it the passage of Time
that has snatched away those years
to douse the fire of adventure
that had kindled all along?
Or is it just me?

I close my eyes
I have come a long way,
crossed many milestones
have been a doting wife and mother,
finally said goodbyes to my children
who have left to find a foothold in this world.

Now, I face an empty nest
that echoes with their childish cries of excitement.
They have flown away like birds from a nest,
      to visit me, just once or twice
      then fly into oblivion.

Life is busy.
          Dear ones
              forgotten.

Unfolding Summer

Cloud mottled sky.
Shadow-flecked Mount Benson,
silver spangled Long lake,
silent sighing creeks,
echo shrill cries of a golden eagle
that resound far and wide.

Sparkling streams meander lazily,
their mercurial waters networking
the lush green fabric of a city called Nanaimo.

Come summer,
bushes, heavy with blueberries and blackberries,
skirt trails that wind through forests of oak
and age old cedars.

Ducks and herons play hide and seek
among the tall swaying bulrushes
pockmarking the still waters of a pond.

Daises smile and nod
through overgrown sword ferns and stinging nettle.

I watch summer's drama unfold ...
     a wish come true.

Waiting For Fall

Something seemed different.
Was it the deep blue of the Lapis lazuli sky?
or the rush of waves in the ocean ?

I felt it in the air,
I felt it echo across the cypress and pine furred hills.
Is it Fall?

I heard your whisper
amidst the boughs of the wispy willow
and the tremulous dance of the maple leaves,
as they twirled like confetti over cushions of air,
turning from pale yellow to ochre.
I saw you with your magic wand,
gently turning lush green valleys
into burnished gold.

Your Midas touch,
fills the air with wispy dandelions,
as a ruddy faced moon hangs limp
in the twilight sky.

I inhale your soft lavender-laced breath
that gently ripples the still waters
of winding streams,
skirting creeks and sharp rocky ridges.

Peaches and apricots are blushed red
and wild bushes bend double
with juicy blackberries,
as kids fill buckets,
while fingers become sticky and purple.

Nobody cares. Shadows lengthen,
gallop across blazing cornfields
tacked to pumpkin patches
and the golden orb of the sun lingers no more.

A veil of darkness wraps the dying day
and the evening star beckons.
Bulrushes nod under a twilight sky
while a family of quails, calls it a day.

                It *is* Fall.

The Tide Of Life

Still summer evening.
The sky, a flushed pink,
blushes at the dying day.
Honey-suckle laced breeze,
sings a dirge to the orb of the scintillating sun,
descending in the distant horizon,
awash with color ...
A tawny sunset.

Twilight sets in
and the day takes a final bow.
A curtain call for sparrows
streaking across the mauve-tinged sky,
their wings tinged gold
with the last rays of the setting sun.

Rolling meadows and valleys echo with shrill cries
of bullfinches and sparrows
returning homeward after their day's sojourn.

Far out in the west,
the ocean lies in deep slumber —
its mercurial waters, a silky sheen
lapping the sandy shore.

All the time, the powdery blue of the mountains
slowly fades into oblivion,
a veil of darkness wrapping around it.

The cycle of life,
comes to a grinding halt.
A distant star beckons.
Seconds become minutes.
Minutes change into hours,
soon to become days
that stretch into months and years.

Vanishing into the Blue

All this, we call Time,
an unsolved mystery with no replay or fast forward.

Life seems a tiny bubble caught in Time's tide.

The hour glass of life runs out
waning, slowly till naught remains.

Where are we in all this?
A tiny cog inTime's machine ?
Or is Life caught in a whirlpool,
that never stops or restarts ?

Is It Really Fall?

Autumn wind,
sighs softly through slender boughs of cherry trees,
ruffles the just blooming pink cherry blossom,
gives a clarion call that Fall is here.

Grey brooding skies,
cool air fans, beaches with swirling sands
stretching into the dreamy blue ocean,
as children play beach ball in the soft dimpled sand.
There is a strange feeling in the air,
as if everything is about to get a make-over.

Hills, like crumpled velvet, turn a rusty brown
       sighing in silence,
speaking a language, unspoken by man.

Cedars, tinted a pale yellow,
the trembling aspen turns russet and gold.
Dogwood leaves are puckered pale.
Fall fairy spreads her magic,
making leaves twirl and dance in little eddies,
as the arbutus nods to the sky
and children dance and sing,
lick lollipops and run after Buster
frisking around, chasing his tail.

A heron hunched on a rail
looks askance at the still waters
of a shimmering pond.

The wind picks up speed,
ruffles the water's glossy surface
into a thousand ripples,
as dusk approaches
and feathery shadows of pines
stretch across the glen.

The wild smell of autumn,
caught by wind-battered elms.

    The sky pales
and the evening star beckons.

Harvest Moon

Twilight ascends
amidst a flush of fading crimson light.
It is neither light nor dark,
when the earth and sky meditate in a silent prayer,
paying obeisance to the silvery orb,
tucked behind a grey tuft of cloud.

The evening star ascends,
a silent salutation to the moon,
etched like a disc on the blackboard of the sky.

Harvest moon,
a puckered orange,
mirrored in a shimmering sheet of water,
whose waves lap up the dusky evening.

       Harvest moon.

In the black hole of a starless night
a weightless orb rises
like a balloon slipping from a girl's hands,
as a cloud mottled sky
says goodbye to the sinking sun,
slipping behind the pines.

A sudden onset of night breeze swaddles the earth
and the clouds drift away.

       There lies the harvest moon,
         its silvery skeins bridging
           earth to infinity.

       A celestial splendour.

Mystic Moon

In the mystic twilight of summer,
I saw you ascend gently,
like Apollo from a chariot of flouncy clouds,
regal and floating in the bosom of the cosmos.

All the while, the earth lay still and quiet,
swaddled by the lavender-laced air,
rocking it gently to sleep.

Skeins of moonlight
spill across silent meadows and sighing hills.
Fern hemmed ponds shimmer silver.
The clatter of crickets and the twitter of sparrows
drowns in the wing flutter of a night jar.

All the time, the blue moon blinks,
surrounded by its starry splendor.
An old barn owl watches,
under a hypnotic spell.

   Mesmerizing.
     Magical.

Crescent Moon

Still silent night.

A dark sky flushes silver with countless stars
forming myriad patterns that blind the eye.

Lonely valleys nestled by braided hills
lie in deep slumber.

All this time, someone watches,
       hanging low,
tags behind the cypress and the shaggy pines,
to sail across hamlets rooted in earthly quiet.

  A halo of light reflects on stately pines,
as a quarter moon hangs limp in the night sky,
     casting a spell on humanity.

Night Watch

Lemony moonlight spills on silent moors,
dotted with clumps of cedars and arbutus
standing as ghostly sentinels
with muted tongues.

At the far end lies a pond,
a shimmering mirror of mercurial waters,
hemmed nettle and furze that rustle and flap
when the cold November wind stirs up,
sweeping through the shaggy fronds of a lone willow.

All the while, a slender moon
keeps a lonely vigil,
as the earth slumbers
under its starry bed.

Hypnotic stillness.
Cicadas fall silent,
save for the sighing of the breeze,
that makes the maple leaves flap and clap
as part of their nightly ritual.

It is time for vespers.

Lo And Behold!

I rise like a phoenix,
among through wispy clouds,
as I sail across the dark heavens.

I flit among the glittering stars
scattered like gems
in the bottomless vault of the sky.
A mute witness to the icy cold night.

A curly haired child looks at me
through his bedroom window.
Awestruck, the child watches,
       unblinking.

Is it a giant ball that floats at night?
Is it an apparition?
Is it a spectre so spectacular
that casts a magic spell?
Is it a fairy come alive from my story book?

Just as the day takes its final bow,
the sky turns a misty mauve,
and the darkness swallows the day
and spills on silent moors.

I rise like a balloon
floating across the muted sky,
I overlook the glow of dim lights
flickering in hamlets,
dotting lonely valleys.

I see flickering shadows
passing grey clouds,
to envelop low lying hills.

I wink and blink
with my half-shut eye,

as a shower of Northern lights,
dances over the starry November night;
and earthlings '*aah* and *ooh*'
held under its hypnotic spell.

Night Sky

A dank and deep vault of darkness
      swaddles the earth,
as we sleep snugly wafted by a lullaby of dreams,
about mist-wrapped distant lands.

      I look up.

Behind the cloak of darkness
there lies a glittering veil
adorning the night sky,
streaking across like a silver shower
that travels across aeons of miles
as meteorites and asteroids whiz past
at speeds that baffle the eye.

Squinting my eyes, I look askance,
the bottomless pit of the sky
is brilliant with swirling lights

Their movement a perfect synchronism
with the motion of the earth.

A curtain of green and florescent band of yellow
lights up in the horizon,
the colors sheer and electric,
melting and melding into one another.

A stunning display of Northern Lights,
dazzling and brilliant,
makes me forget myself.

      Who am I ?

The Breath Of Autumn

I stand atop a hill
on an early morn
and hear your beacon call —
your balmy breath,
as you whisper sweet nothings
to the stately pines and conifers.

You fly with your invisible cape
rustling through their slender branches,
to make stately willows dance and sway.

You gently rise, your breath a soft lullaby,
as you transform maple trees
from green to ochre to a flaming red,
setting hillsides ablaze
with the fiery plumes of cedars.

      You ascend to the grey sky,
        to make wispy clouds
play hide and seek with the setting sun.

You send ripples through still waters of ponds,
making them glisten like a thousand prisms
bathed in the brilliance of a Fall morning.

Come dusk,
you blow harder
and the leaves of the sprawling oak tree
pirouette and glide in the air
like little ballerinas
    then sink
onto the ground below.

A family of furry squirrels
scurries down the rugged trunk
of the old dogwood tree,
to nosedive into a pile

of crinkled yellow leaves
that were once skittering down
the cobbled sidewalk.

Welcome autumn.

Wintry Dusk

Scarlet sky.
Wrapped in a cocoon of snow,
the village lies tucked in, skirting the valley.

Last rays of the feeble winter sun
bathe the deserted snow-rutted lanes
and rooftops with a soft rosy glow,
as it slowly sinks to rest.

Faint lights glimmer through frilly curtains
of bedroom windows ,
warm with the glowing hearths.

A delectable smell of a cauldron,
bubbling with chicken soup
whets the appetite of menfolk
who have toiled hard and long,
to call it a day and raise a glass of wine.

      A toast to winter.

Down the bend lies a still pond,
edged with piles and piles of snow
      that fell last night.
  Its water frosty and crusted.
Bulrushes sway, bent heavy
with the weight of snow
that lies like fluffy meringue.

A solitary horse-cart clatters past.
A cool breeze stirs up from the west
while a lone star watches, unblinking
     in the cold firmament.

The First Snowfall

The first snowfall –
a landscape painted crystal white,
luminescent in a silence so eerie.

A hush echoing across the silent valleys.

Fog smothered fields lie in front of me
as a cold wind picks up speed.
Its low hum rises in crescendo ,
howling through the bony skeleton of arbutus
and the slender frame of cypress,
once enrobed in leafy green.

Last rays of the setting sun,
fall askance on a snow-rutted path,
silhouette a grove of pine trees,
sending slender shadows galloping
toward the blurry horizon.

A family of wild geese
pockmark the tawny sky in the west,
as they fly into oblivion —
to their home so far away.

Look To This Day!

In the fading of the setting sun,
arched street lamps line like soldiers
on a deserted snow carpeted winding road,
      leading to
an unknown destination.

   Bony branches of arbutus
       intertwine above,
a bower for the dancing snowflakes
     that twirl and swirl
     in the frigid cold air,
       then sink ...
     to the frozen ground
       with a flourish.

The air is crackling,
flecked with fresh snowfall.
Warm glow of yellow street lights
sends angular shadows slanting across,
to straddle over to the frosty grass
reflecting a mosaic
of tiny rainbows come to earth.

Yellow warblers dart like shot arrows,
      through the cypress,
     on their way home.

     The river is crimson
with the sun melting into its calm waters,
   to sink till a narrow cusp remains.

I say goodbye,
as I sit sipping hot latte,
curls of steam arise,
melt into the air
just as the sun is visible no more.

A day is done,

Tomorrow will be another day,
    a new life,
      a new world.

An Evening To Remember

     Solemn Fall evening.
The pale sun veiled by a grey cloud,
       a soft blur.

A slate-grey squirrel
frisks on the leaf speckled grass,
its eyes desperately searching for acorns;
then darts into a wild bramble bush,
its furry tail still in sight.

Feeble sunlight filters through our maple tree,
   once a luxuriant green,
now a splash of golden yellow.

A russet sun bids au revoir to the dying day,
     as a gentle breeze
ripples through the stately cypress trees
   standing like sentinels in prayer.

       The breeze dies down
     leaving the leaves muted
      in hushed expectancy.

    The magnetic pull of stillness.

Night awaits in the wings of twilight,
fazed colors of Fall come alive in vivid splendour,
just before the first star twinkles awake.

Grey sky broods over a filigree of poplar branches,
     leafless and naked,
as a cold wind rips through them.

A golden eagle's nest sits precariously
on a stubbly branch of a silver birch,
     empty and soulless.

Down below, winds a road
skirted by shaggy headed pines
standing like mute sentinels.

A black Porsche zips past,
its taillights flashing red,
swallowed into the fold of approaching darkness.

A few yards ahead is a bus stop
with a rundown dented signboard,
a place where school kids with satchels
wait for the bright yellow school bus,
resounding with the endless chatter
      of boys and girls.

     Straight ahead,
   as far as the eye can see,
fluffy clouds float lazily above the horizon
    veiled by the twilight mist
floating gently over the still waters of the ocean,
     so tranquil.

The Pulse Of Winter

Grey leaden sky
broods over silent hills,
fur-coated with conical cypress that taper
among a tangled matrix of arbutus and sprawling cedars.

    A veil of wintry mist
floats from the ruffled visage of the ocean.

    It is winter.

The air, still and spooky.
    Soundless.

Deep and mysterious forests slumber,
   lost in dreams of far-off lands
  awash in the mellow winter sun.

Still Summer Sky

Still summer sky
bows toward auzure blue mountains
that gently arise,
veiled by the evening mist.

Down below,
rows upon rows
of conifers stand like sentinels
lining the silvery façade of the ocean,
    so smooth and silky.

A painting come to life —
the cloudless sky, its canvas
etched with sweeping grey
silhouettes of mountains,
splashed with verdant
and sap green of the trees
and the mercurial glow
of the aquamarine ocean.

    Who is the Artist
and where is His brush?

The First Blush

A rose-hued sky
colors the canvas of the winter evening,
pockmarked with snow dusted conifers,
standing like silent sentinels.

The ground, a white carpet
pugmarked with hoof-prints,
maybe from a doe-eyed deer
that has strayed away from its home.

The sun is setting into twilight
tinting the horizon a misty lavender,
casting a magic spell.

Silvery skeins of twilight
usher in the soft starry veil of night.
Evening breeze, laced with honeysuckle, stirs up,
      heralding a crescent moon;
         a wisp of a comma
      hanging limp in the sky.

I hear a rustle in a closeby wild berry bush.

      A night bird calls,
heralding the solitude of the evening —
      this sacred hour.

Magic Of A Summer Night

Summer night sky.
A starry veil wraps the somnolent earth in its bosom.

Sighing valleys,
nestled among silent wooded hills
arise like crest and tufts of waves
swallowed in the inky darkness.

A few lights twinkle with a mellow glow,
perhaps those of a few farmers' houses
       huddled together
with thatched barns tacked to them.

       Far below,
  flows a meandering river —
a silvery thread of mercurial waters
weaving though rocky creeks and cliffs.

       Up above,
a golden eagle soars in circles,
    looking for its prey.

Vanishing Into The Blue

We come into this world
with a clean slate.
Our book, empty and bare.

We write, chapter after chapter
from day to day,
from hour to hour,
each page becoming a lived memory.

A mosaic of colorful joys
and dark tearful sorrows,
of the mundane and the unexpected,
that lie hidden;
of losses and gains and more.

Page after page is written.

>Though my pen falters .
>I never stop
> as the last chapter
>needs to be completed
> and an epilogue
>is not to be forgotten.

There are no edits or polishing here,
    no rewrites or deletes.

  Time ticks by relentlessly,
and Life vanishes into the blue.

    Who will read my book?
Who will make memories come alive?

      I know not ...

      I know not

www.ingramcontent.com/pod-product-compliance
Lightning Source LLC
Chambersburg PA
CBHW071320080526
44587CB00018B/3300